MAR 2 2 2016

MAR 2 2 2016

TO THE RESCUE!

GARRETT MORGAN
UNDERGROUND

Monica Kulling   *Illustrated by David Parkins*

TUNDRA BOOKS

For Lisa and Robert,
with love and gratitude for your support
M.K.

Tundra Books, a division of Random House of Canada Limited, a
Penguin Random House Company

Library and Archives Canada Cataloguing in Publication

Kulling, Monica, 1952–, author
       To the rescue! : Garrett Morgan underground / written by
Monica Kulling; illustrated by David Parkins.

(Great idea series)
Includes bibliographical references.
Issued in print and electronic formats.
ISBN 978-1-77049-520-3 (bound).–ISBN 978-1-77049-521-0 (epub)

       1. Morgan, Garrett A., 1877–1963 – Juvenile literature.
2. African American inventors – Biography – Juvenile literature.
3. Breathing apparatus – Juvenile literature. I. Parkins, David,
illustrator II. Title. III. Series: Great idea series

T40.M67K84 2016   j609.2   C2014-905500-5
                                          C2014-905501-3

Published simultaneously in the United States of America by Tundra
Books of Northern New York, a division of Random House of Canada
Limited, a Penguin Random House Company

Library of Congress Control Number: 2014951822

Sources of inspiration:

Evans, Harold, with Gail Buckland and David Lefer. *They Made
America: From the Steam Engine to the Search Engine*. New York:
Back Bay Books/Little Brown and Company, 2004.

Murphy, Patricia J. *Garrett Morgan: Inventor of the Traffic Light and
Gas Mask*. New Jersey: Enslow Publishers, Inc., 2004.

Oluonye, Mary N. *Garrett Augustus Morgan: Businessman, Inventor,
Good Citizen*. Ohio: AuthorHouse, 2008.

Sullivan, Otha Richard. *African American Inventors*. New Jersey:
John Wiley & Sons, Inc., 1998.

Internet:

http://inventors.about.com/od/mstartinventors/a/Garrett_Morgan.
htm

http://www.biography.com/people/garrett-morgan-9414691

Edited by Sue Tate
Designed by Leah Springate
The artwork in this book was rendered in pen and ink with watercolor
on paper.
The text was set in Minion.
Printed and bound in China

www.penguinrandomhouse.ca

1   2   3   4   5   20   19   18   17   16

Underground

Try to imagine
what it must be like
far underground
in the deep dank earth

Think of the worms
and burrowing moles
that live in the gloom
unafraid of the dark

Think of the men
lowered on ropes
to underground tunnels
where disaster can strike

The Kentucky fields were sunbaked. Families worked in the blazing heat of the day. Come harvest time, they would share their crops with the landowner. It was a hardscrabble life.

Garrett Morgan's parents had once been slaves. They were free now, but the family still worked the fields as hard as ever.

One day, Garrett stopped hoeing to stretch. *I want more than this*, he thought, gazing at the worn-out farm he'd lived on all his life.

Garrett Augustus Morgan was born in 1877 in Paris, Kentucky. He was the seventh of eleven children. Each one labored in the fields from the time they could hold a hoe.

Garrett left school at a young age. He wanted to earn a living, but he had only two choices: work on the land or on the railroad. Garrett didn't want to do either, so, at fourteen, he headed north to seek his fortune.

In 1895, Garrett was settled in Cleveland, Ohio. As he swept floors in a clothing factory, he noticed that the belts on the sewing machines often broke. Garrett decided to make a stronger belt.

When he did, the boss was so pleased that he gave Garrett a new job – sewing-machine repairman. Garrett was on his way!

By 1908, Garrett had his own house and sewing-machine shop. Soon he and his wife, Mary Anne, opened a tailoring shop too.

One day, in his home workshop, Garrett was concocting a cream to prevent sewing-machine needles from making scorch marks in fabric. Little did he know that he was about to stumble upon his first invention.

At the end of the day, Garrett wiped his cream-covered hands on a piece of woolen cloth. By morning, the fuzzy threads of the cloth were smooth and straight. Amazing!

"I've got an idea," Garrett said to Mary Anne, with a twinkle in his eye.

"Not on *my* curls, you don't," she replied.

Garrett decided to try his invention on his neighbor's dog, an Airedale terrier. Airedales have tightly curled hair, not fur. The cream worked! The neighbor didn't recognize his own dog!

At bedtime, Garrett coated his own hair with the cream. By morning, his hair was smooth and straight.

Garrett patented his invention in 1910. He called it a hair refiner. He called his new business the G. A. Morgan Hair Refining Company.

Garrett made other hair-care products too, such as a dye called Black Oil Hair Stain, a hair grower, and a curved-tooth comb to straighten hair.

Garrett's hair products sold well. With the money he made, he was able to spend more time on his true passion – inventing.

In 1911, a shocking story hit the front pages of America's newspapers. The Triangle Shirtwaist Factory in New York City had caught fire, and 146 workers were dead. Most of them were teenage girls.

Over breakfast, Garrett read the headline aloud: "WOMEN AND GIRLS, TRAPPED IN TEN STORY BUILDING, LOST IN FLAMES OR HURL THEMSELVES TO DEATH."

Fires were common in cities, where many buildings were made of wood. After the Great Chicago Fire of 1871 had killed hundreds, destroying homes and businesses, it took years for workers to rebuild the city.

When firefighters entered a burning building, they were often overcome by smoke. It was difficult for them to rescue those who were trapped inside.

Garrett decided to invent a hood to give firefighters a fighting chance.

Once, at a circus, Garrett saw an elephant reach its long trunk out the tent flap to breathe fresh air. This gave him an idea. In a fire, smoke, dust and poisonous gases rise. The air at ground level is breathable.

Garrett's safety hood, the forerunner of the gas mask, included a long tube that reached to the ground, just like an elephant's trunk. A second tube allowed the user to exhale air. A wet sponge filtered out smoke and cooled the air.

The hood was made of fireproof canvas. Garrett called his invention Morgan's Safety Hood and Smoke Protector.

Garrett tested his hood to make sure it did exactly what he wanted it to do. When he burned chemicals in a tent, the enclosed area was soon thick with smoke.

Garrett walked into the tent wearing his safety hood. He stayed for twenty long minutes. He didn't cough or faint. Garrett was able to breathe, just like the elephant in the circus tent. The hood worked!

Garrett filed for a patent for this invention in 1914.

Sales of the safety hood were disappointing. Garrett sold one or two to fire departments, but most people weren't interested in buying it when they found out its inventor was Black.

In America's South, Garrett hired a white man who pretended to be "Mr. Morgan," while *he* acted as his assistant.

Then, one day, a disaster put Garrett's invention onto the front pages of the newspapers.

The tunnel was filling fast with smoke, dust, and poisonous gas. None of the rescuers could stay down long enough to see where they were going. It looked like the trapped men were doomed.

Suddenly one of them remembered seeing Garrett Morgan demonstrate his invention. "We need Garrett Morgan's Safety Hood!" he exclaimed.

Men raced to Garrett's home to wake him up. Garrett brought his brother Frank and four hoods, or "gas masks," to the scene.

Garrett, Frank, and two other men entered the tunnel.
Would the masks work? Was it too late to save anyone?

Garrett slowly emerged, pulling out one of the workers.
He was alive! Frank came up with another. The masks worked!
One by one, the rescuers saved as many men as they could.

Soon, police and fire departments across the country
were ordering Morgan's Safety Hood. The city of Cleveland
honored Garrett with a gold medal for his heroic efforts.

Garrett's invention, developed further, would save
thousands of soldiers from chlorine gas in the trenches of
World War I.

Safety First

In the early days of the automobile, there were no traffic signals. Drivers drove wherever they found room on the road among pedestrians, bicycles, and animal-drawn wagons. Intersections were especially dangerous.

Garrett was the first African-American in Cleveland to own a car. One day, while driving, he witnessed a horrible crash between a car and a horse-drawn carriage. He couldn't get the accident out of his mind. Garrett was convinced he could do something to improve traffic safety, so he invented a traffic signal device.

Garrett's device was a T-shaped pole that featured three positions: Stop, Go, and All-Stop. The All-Stop signal stopped traffic in all directions so that pedestrians could safely cross the roads.

Garrett Morgan was one of the earliest inventors to apply for and acquire a patent for a traffic signal. He had come to the rescue once again.